ALIEN PSYCHOLOGY
How to Prepare for the Existence of Extraterrestrial Life

Christian Druso
Gistain Montolío

Index

INTRODUCTION

In an infinitely vast and ever-expanding universe, the possibility that we are not alone has been an enigma that has ignited the curiosity and imagination of humanity since ancient times. We live in an era where everything known is changing at a dizzying pace. Nothing remains as it once was. Scientific advancements, particularly in technology, are progressing at such rapid speeds that what is conceived today can become obsolete within months. Trends and fads are increasingly fleeting, and the immediacy of everything has become a societal demand.

Perhaps the setting isn't the most fitting, but if there were ever a moment considered optimal for disclosing the existence of extraterrestrial life to humanity, I dare say it is now. And by this, I don't refer to current circumstances, but rather to the mental characteristics of the middle-aged population inhabiting planet Earth. I venture to claim that those born between 1970 and 2000 are the ones who have experienced the most drastic changes and therefore might possess greater openness and mental readiness to assimilate news or novelties that could have a significant impact on their lives. Despite not having predominantly experienced wartime situations, they have been in a state of almost constant adaptation to change. Even certain premises, concepts, or values that were once considered steadfast and certain have undergone variations in recent times. Tolerance for frustration and resilience are among their skills, resources that the younger generation seems not to possess. For these reasons, I believe we are the last generation capable of confronting the greatest mental impact ever experienced. The communication of extraterrestrial life's existence should occur now.

In fact, if we heed the news, the concept of extraterrestrial life is no longer confined to the realm of science fiction; it holds prospects of becoming a tangible and real possibility.

This book is an attempt to explain how to confront the revelation of extraterrestrial life's existence from a psychological and sociological perspective. As scientific advancements and physical evidence bring us closer to the possibility of discovering beings beyond our planet, a series of questions arise that extend beyond mere biological existence. How will this revelation impact our beliefs, our perception of humanity, and our relationship with the cosmos?

In the following pages, after briefly examining the similarities and differences between ancient myths and modern theories and uncovering how speculation about extraterrestrials has persisted throughout human history, I will delve into the recesses of the human psyche. I will explore various emotional reactions that could emerge upon receiving the news that we are not alone in the universe. I will review how our cultural, religious, and philosophical history intertwines with the possibility of extraterrestrial life and how these elements have shaped our perception of "other beings."

I will dare to venture into the depths of individual and collective psychology to unravel how encounters with the unknown, whether real or perceived, could have influenced the mental well-being of those involved. Above all, I will offer guidance on how we should confront the challenges that lie ahead. How can we prepare ourselves mentally and emotionally to face a reality that challenges our traditional conceptions? How can we address the uncertainty and change that may arise from this cosmic discovery?

From an individual standpoint and with entirely personal opinions presented here, I hope that readers find in this manuscript a beam of light that, in addition to being captivating due to its content's nature, can illuminate their path toward a future where humanity approaches a potential extraordinary encounter with the extraterrestrial.

CHAPTER 1

A brief history of speculation about extraterrestrial life

In this first chapter, I have deemed it essential to provide a brief historical overview of how the notion of life beyond Earth has been a part of human culture since our origins as a species.

Throughout ancient times, humanity has gazed at the sky and pondered whether we were alone in the universe. The idea of the potential existence of extraterrestrial life has been ingrained in human culture throughout its history, expressed through myths, legends, religions, art, and philosophy.

Mythology and Ancient Religion:

In ancient civilizations, myths and religions offered explanations for celestial phenomena. Many cultures believed that gods inhabited the heavens or other planets, such as the Egyptian and Mesopotamian gods. The notion that some of these gods might have been extraterrestrial or representatives of beings from other planets is a modern interpretation, grounded in certain similarities that could be found between certain mythological accounts and concepts associated with the possibility of extraterrestrial life.

For example, one might observe specific descriptions in which gods descended from the sky or rode in "chariots" traversing the heavens. Similarly, iconography from these civilizations may depict beings with non-human features, sometimes wearing peculiar helmets or devices that could be interpreted as advanced technology. In ancient Egypt, certain Egyptian reliefs and hieroglyphs could be construed as potential depictions of beings not native to Earth. In fact, representations of beings with animal heads, like the god Horus, could be interpreted as humanoid extraterrestrial entities.

In Sumerian civilization (one of the earliest known civilizations), certain myths such as the Epic of Gilgamesh might suggest interactions between extraterrestrial deities and humans. The Epic of Gilgamesh, an ancient epic poem dating back to around the 3rd millennium BCE, is among humanity's oldest known literary works. Originating in ancient Mesopotamia, in the region now corresponding to Iraq, the story centers on the Sumerian king Gilgamesh, who ruled in the city of Uruk, and his quest for immortality. Various interpretations suggest that these characters and their relationship with celestial divinities might represent alliances with extraterrestrial beings. The divine origin of Gilgamesh (a king with both human and divine parts), the arrival of Enkidu, Gilgamesh's friend and adventure companion, a wild man created by the gods to balance Gilgamesh's power, the journey to the abode of the gods atop a mountain where a goddess, Siduri, resides in the "garden of the gods," a place of potential extraterrestrial origin.

In Mayan culture, some hieroglyphs and murals have been interpreted by researchers as depictions of extraterrestrial beings. These interpretations are rooted in figures displaying non-human characteristics or in flying objects that could suggest the presence of beings from other worlds.

The Dogon culture of West Africa stands out for its detailed knowledge of the Sirius star system. This has led to speculation that their knowledge might have been acquired through ancient contacts with extraterrestrial beings.

In sacred texts like the Bible, celestial beings and mysterious creatures are mentioned, suggesting the existence of life beyond Earth. Specifically, in the Old Testament of the Bible, several celestial beings, such as angels and seraphim, are mentioned. Angels are described as divine messengers who act as intermediaries between God and humans, possessing clearly supernatural attributes. In fact, certain biblical passages, like the book of Ezekiel in the Old Testament, contain symbolic descriptions and enigmatic visions that could be interpreted as encounters with extraterrestrial beings. Known as "The Vision of the Wheels" or "The Chariot of Fire," it is found in chapter 1, verses 4 to 28. Here is a summary of some key points from the passage:

Ezekiel, a prophet of the Babylonian exile, describes a vision he had while by the River Chebar. In his vision, he sees a tempestuous wind coming from the north and a great cloud with flashing fire and a bright glow around it. In the midst of the cloud, there are four living creatures with peculiar appearances: each has four faces (human, lion, ox, and eagle) and four wings. Additionally, these beings have human hands beneath their wings. Beside each of these beings are wheels that move alongside them and have a structure resembling wheels within wheels. The wheels gleam like topaz and are full of eyes. These wheels appear alive and move in perfect coordination with the living creatures. When the beings move, the wheels move; when the beings stop, the wheels stop as well. Furthermore, above the heads of the beings and above the firmament over their heads, Ezekiel sees something resembling brilliant blue crystal. And above the firmament, he sees the appearance of a sapphire throne, upon which there is a human-like figure surrounded by a fiery radiance. Ezekiel describes this human-like figure as encompassed by a rainbow.

Classical Philosophy:

Democritus (460 BCE - 370 BCE) was a pre-Socratic philosopher and one of the earliest thinkers to develop the atomic theory, which posited that everything in the universe was composed of indivisible and perpetually moving atoms. He believed in an infinite number of worlds, an idea related to his concept of the universe as an infinite collection of atoms in perpetual motion within infinite space. In this view, each conceivable combination of atoms would result in a unique world. His idea of countless worlds inhabited by different combinations of atoms could be construed as a suggestion of the possibility of other forms of life in the cosmos.

Renaissance (14th-16th Century):

During the Renaissance, the idea of inhabited worlds gained momentum due to the growing understanding of the solar system and the realization that Earth was not the center of the universe. Giordano Bruno (1548-1600) was a prominent Italian Dominican friar, philosopher, and Renaissance thinker who became one of the earliest known proponents of the idea of countless inhabited worlds in the cosmos. His ideas deviated from the prevailing geocentric and theocentric view of his time, advocating for an infinite universe replete with Earth-like worlds. Influenced by Copernicus' ideas, Bruno championed the heliocentric theory, asserting that Earth and planets revolved around the Sun, rather than Earth serving as the center of the universe. This perspective challenged the traditional geocentric view and suggested that Earth was neither unique nor exceptional in the cosmos. Additionally, he contended that the universe was infinitely expansive, filled with innumerable stars and planets, each of which could harbor life. Similarly, he espoused a panpsychic philosophy, proposing that consciousness existed in all things, including stars and planets. This animistic perspective led him to consider that life and intelligence could manifest anywhere within the universe. Furthermore, unlike the anthropocentric outlook prevailing in his time that deemed Earth and humanity the center of creation, Bruno advocated for a more humble view of humanity's place in the cosmos. He believed that life and intelligence were not exclusive to Earth and existed in other worlds. Notably, his ideas were also influenced by hermetic and esoteric concepts, which emphasized the idea of a universe populated by spiritual and divine beings. These esoteric notions bolstered his belief in a plurality of inhabited worlds. Understandably, due to his controversial ideas and his departure from the traditional perspectives held by both Church and science of the time, Bruno faced persecution and charges of heresy by the Inquisition. He was ultimately sentenced to the stake and executed in 1600. Though his legacy and ideas were suppressed in his era, Giordano Bruno is remembered as a bold and visionary thinker who pushed the boundaries of contemporary thought, paving the way for a broader understanding of the universe and the possibility of extraterrestrial life. Today, he is recognized as a martyr of free thought and freedom of expression.

20th Century and the Science Fiction Era:

H.G. Wells and Jules Verne were two of the most influential authors in 19th and early 20th-century science fiction literature. Both envisioned interplanetary journeys and encounters with extraterrestrial beings in their works, though their approaches and styles differed. H.G. Wells, in his novel "The War of the Worlds" (1898), provided one of the earliest instances of an alien invasion in literature. It narrates the arrival of Martians, highly technologically advanced extraterrestrial beings, who launch a devastating invasion of Earth. The novel portrays humanity's desperate struggle against an unrelenting extraterrestrial race and their destructive war machines.

On the other hand, Jules Verne's "From the Earth to the Moon" (1865) tells the story of a group of men who construct an enormous cannon to launch a projectile to the Moon. Although the journey does not involve direct encounters with extraterrestrial beings, the novel is an early example of human imagination exploring and colonizing other worlds.

20th Century, Space Age, and the Search for Life:

In the 20th century, the possibility of extraterrestrial life became a serious scientific question. Since then, various programs to search for extraterrestrial life have been developed, spanning scientific initiatives, radio astronomy projects, and space missions. Below is a brief summary of some notable programs:

The Search for Extraterrestrial Intelligence (SETI) Project: Initiated in 1960 by astronomer Frank Drake, the SETI Project has evolved over the years across various institutions and organizations. Its primary goal is to search for electromagnetic signals that might indicate possible extraterrestrial intelligence. These signals are mainly sought within the radio and microwave range.

NASA Space Missions: NASA has conducted several space missions that explore planets and moons in search of evidence of past or present life. Missions like Viking (Mars), Galileo (Jupiter), Cassini-Huygens (Saturn and its moons), and more recently, the Perseverance rover (Mars), are designed to search for traces of life and gain a better understanding of conditions for habitability on other celestial bodies.

Hubble Space Telescope and Other Space Telescopes: The Hubble Space Telescope has been used to study exoplanets (planets outside our solar system) and their atmospheres in search of signs of life. Additionally, other space telescopes such as the Spitzer Space Telescope and the upcoming James Webb Space Telescope have also contributed to this research. The discovery of exoplanets in the past decade has led to the notion that there could be billions of Earth-like planets in the Milky Way galaxy. Consequently, the identification of habitable zones around nearby stars has expanded the possibilities of finding planets that could harbor life.

Breakthrough Listen Project: Initiated in 2015 and funded by Russian billionaire Yuri Milner, the Breakthrough Listen Project is one of the largest and most ambitious programs to search for extraterrestrial life to date. It employs powerful telescopes and radio astronomy equipment to track extraterrestrial signals and study nearby stars.

ESA Exploration Missions: The European Space Agency (ESA) has also engaged in exploration and the search for extraterrestrial life. For example, the Rosetta spacecraft studied the comet 67P/Churyumov-Gerasimenko to gather clues about the origins of life.

Arecibo Project: The Arecibo Observatory, located in Puerto Rico, was a project that utilized a massive radio telescope to search for extraterrestrial signals from 1963 until its collapse in 2020.

Naturally, as technology and science continue to advance, it is likely that more initiatives will be developed in the future to address the captivating question of whether we are alone in the universe.

CHAPTER 2

Artistic representations and artworks related to the extraterrestrial phenomenon

Something that has always captured my attention is the diverse artistic representations that, throughout history, might depict elements not of terrestrial origin or that deviate from the temporal sequence we currently accept as true. Let us not forget that human beings began their pictorial representations by reproducing images they encountered in their daily lives.

The paintings of the Wondjina or Wandjina are a collection of Aboriginal rock art (174,000 BCE) found in caves and rocky spaces in the Kimberley region, north of Australia. These paintings hold significant cultural and spiritual importance for the Aboriginal peoples of the region. The depictions of Wondjina often feature humanoid figures with large round eyes, narrow mouths, and frequently lacking noses or ears. They possess a distinctive and ethereal appearance that could be interpreted as hints of extraterrestrial beings. For the Aboriginal peoples of the Kimberley region, Wondjina are ancestral and powerful spiritual beings considered the creators of the earth, sky, and living creatures. These paintings are a form of sacred art, believed to possess spiritual and protective power over the land and its inhabitants. It is important to note that Australian Aboriginal perspectives on extraterrestrial beings differ from Western interpretations, and they do not regard Wondjina as representations of extraterrestrial entities.

Similarly, in 2014, a cave was discovered in India containing cave paintings dating back over 10,000 years. These paintings prominently feature figures with shapes remarkably resembling what we understand as UFOs and aliens. According to local archaeologist JR Bhagat, "This could mean that humans in ancient times saw or imagined beings that came from other planets. We need further research. Our department lacks experts in this field." Legends among local tribes tell stories of the "little people" who used to arrive in flying objects and would take one or two tribe members with them. The "abducted" individuals never returned. Interestingly, these oddly shaped figures seem to carry objects resembling weapons, lack detailed facial features, and lack noses and mouths, similar to the Australian case.

In the region of Utah (United States), a series of paintings can also be found in the "Barrier Canyon Rock Art" area. These ancient rock paintings, dating back thousands of years, are considered a form of prehistoric art created by indigenous cultures that inhabited the region in the past. One of their most striking features is their anthropomorphic style, with figures that are often schematic and stylized, possessing elongated bodies and limbs, large eyes and mouths, while others lack facial features, matching the descriptions mentioned earlier.

In this way, we can say that petroglyphs and pictograms that date back several thousand years have been found in different parts of the world, belonging to cultures that had no connection with one another. Yet, they reflect a consistent depiction that could be interpreted as possible UFOs or extraterrestrial beings.

However, there are paintings that captured my attention from a young age when I studied them in my Art History class. These include "The Madonna with Saint John the Baptist" by Italian artist Domenico Ghirlandaio (1449-1494), "The Annunciation with Saint Emidius" by Italian artist Carlo Crivelli (1435-1495), and "The Baptism of Christ" by Dutch artist Aert de Gelder (1645-1727).

The first of these is an Italian Renaissance painting depicting the Virgin Mary with the infant Jesus in her arms and a man looking towards the sky, where a clearly disc-shaped object is visible. The second painting shows a luminous and rounded object in the sky emitting a beam of light during the Annunciation to the Virgin Mary. The third is a Baroque painting from 1710, depicting the Baptism of Christ, with the figure of God represented by a shining object in the sky, clearly displaying the characteristic oval shape of UFOs.

There are more paintings, tapestries, and artistic representations from different countries that contain elements that could be interpreted as extraterrestrial in nature. I invite the reader to conduct their own investigations.

CHAPTER 3

Scientific hypotheses regarding extraterrestrial life

There are several scientific hypotheses regarding the possible existence of extraterrestrial life. Below, I briefly present some of the main ones.

Hypothesis of Microbial Life: This hypothesis suggests that it's possible to find microscopic forms of life, such as bacteria or microorganisms, in other parts of the universe. It's based on the idea that suitable conditions for life, such as liquid water and organic compounds, could exist on other planets or moons.

Hypothesis of Panspermia: According to this hypothesis, life on Earth could have originated from microorganisms or biological material that arrived from other planets or star systems. Asteroid or comet impacts could have transported these organisms to Earth and seeded life on our planet.

Hypothesis of Extremophiles: This hypothesis focuses on the ability of certain living organisms to adapt and survive in extreme conditions. Extremophiles are known organisms on Earth that can survive in highly hostile environments, such as those with high temperatures, pressures, or extreme chemical conditions. Therefore, similar forms of life could exist on other planets with such extreme conditions.

Hypothesis of BioSignatures: This hypothesis is based on the detection of bio-signatures, which are indirect evidence of the existence of life on other planets. Bio-signatures can include the detection of chemical compounds or atmospheric patterns that suggest the presence of biological activity, such as the presence of oxygen in a planetary atmosphere or the ancient presence of water.

Hypothesis of Intelligent Life: This hypothesis proposes the possibility of intelligent and technologically advanced life forms existing elsewhere in the universe. It's based on the idea that given the number of planets in the galaxy and the age of the universe, it's likely that extraterrestrial civilizations capable of developing technology and interstellar communication exist.

Hypothesis of Unconventional Life Forms: This hypothesis suggests that extraterrestrial life could be based on radically different life forms than those we know on Earth. Instead of using carbon as the fundamental element for life, they could use other elements such as silicon or nitrogen in their molecular structures. Moreover, they could have unique metabolisms and biochemical processes. This hypothesis proposes the possibility of exotic and unconventional life forms that significantly differ from life as we know it. Thus, life wouldn't necessarily be limited to the conditions and elements we know on Earth. The universe is vast and diverse, and there could be a wide range of possibilities for life, even beyond our current conceptions.

However, it's in this part of the book that I find it opportune to mention the Fermi Paradox posed in 1950 by Italian physicist Enrico Fermi. This paradox refers to the apparent contradiction between the high probability of extraterrestrial civilizations existing in the universe and the supposed lack of evidence or direct contact with such civilizations. We can summarize it as follows:

The universe contains billions of galaxies, each with billions of stars, many of which are believed to have planetary systems. This suggests that there could be countless planets in the "habitable zone" where conditions might be suitable for life as we know it.

Given the potentially high number of habitable planets, it seems likely that life could emerge on some of them, even if it's rare.

Despite the probability of extraterrestrial life, we have not yet found any conclusive evidence of the existence of extraterrestrial civilizations or received communication signals from them.

For these reasons, the question arises: if there are so many opportunities for extraterrestrial life, why haven't we detected any signals or evidence of its existence? This has led to a series of theories and speculations about possible reasons behind this apparent lack of contact, ranging from the possibility that civilizations might self-destruct before they can communicate to the idea that we simply aren't looking in the right places or in the right ways. However, it's worth noting that Enrico Fermi's assumption of a lack of conclusive evidence may be flawed, as such evidence could have been concealed by governments for centuries. This endeavor of concealment is such a monumental effort that it has not always succeeded in achieving its goals, since despite attempts to discredit individuals who share information related to this topic, experiences and narratives from those involved in such matters do exist.

CHAPTER 4

Why does the human mind feel fascination with extraterrestrial beings?

As a psychologist, the first premise I found relevant to consider is that there is a predisposition in some human beings to feel a certain fascination with extraterrestrial beings. This phenomenon can be attributed to a combination of psychological, sociocultural, and scientific factors.

In this way, extraterrestrial beings represent the unknown and the unexplored. The possibility of the existence of other forms of intelligent life beyond our planet sparks our curiosity and invites us to explore the boundaries of our knowledge.

Similarly, it could provide answers to fundamental questions about our origin, our place in the universe, and whether we are alone in the cosmos. The quest for answers to these existential questions fuels our fascination and leads us to reflect on our own humanity. The idea of extraterrestrial beings can also ignite our search for connection and meaning in the universe. We ponder the existence of other civilizations and how we might interact with them, which prompts us to consider our place in a broader cosmic context.

This brings us to the next point: contemplating our own human condition and our unique characteristics. We wonder what these beings might be like, how they would compare to us, and whether they share fundamental similarities or differences. This process helps us better understand who we are and what makes us human.

Let's not forget that humans are by nature explorative, speculative, and above all, creative beings. The existence of extraterrestrial beings precisely allows us to explore and speculate about a variety of possibilities. We can envision advanced civilizations, futuristic technologies, and exotic life forms, which stimulate our imagination and fuel our creativity.

As a result of this creativity, we have a history of popular culture that, including movies, books, television series, and video games, has played a significant role in spreading this fascination with extraterrestrial beings. These portrayals in the media have contributed to the creation of archetypes and stereotypes of extraterrestrials, influencing our perception and expectations of them.

Naturally, just like in all personal life stories that are unique and diverse, this fascination with extraterrestrial beings may vary in each individual and be influenced by their education, personal experiences, cultural beliefs, and social context. What I have no doubt about is that exploring the possibility of extraterrestrial life poses a unique challenge that compels us to broaden our horizons and reflect on our place in the universe—one of the greatest questions of our species.

CHAPTER 5

Psychological factors influencing belief in extraterrestrials

Similarly, I decided to explore the psychological factors that may influence belief in extraterrestrial beings.

Firstly, this belief, akin to many world religions, can provide a sense of meaning and purpose for individuals. Faced with the vastness of the universe and unanswered questions about our place in it, the idea that we are not alone can offer comfort and a sense of connection to something greater—a belonging to something so immense that our minds cannot fully grasp but can feel.

In fact, religions and spirituality often promote the notion of a vast and wondrous universe created by a higher force. The search for extraterrestrial life could be seen as a way to expand our understanding of divine creation and appreciate the immensity and complexity of the cosmos. However, the possibility of alien life challenges the traditional notion that humans are the center of the universe and unique in existence. This could lead to a reevaluation of religious and spiritual teachings that place humans as the most significant creation. Some religions might need to adapt and reinterpret their teachings to accommodate the possibility of extraterrestrial life, fostering an enriching dialogue between science and religion. It could ultimately serve as a new common ground for both, a reconciliation of these two perspectives. This, in turn, could promote a broader view of humanity and belief in the interconnection of all life forms in the universe—a manifestation of a broader divine design that leads to an opportunity for forging bonds and better understanding our relationship with other intelligent beings. Going even further, the existence of extraterrestrial life might prompt people to wonder if extraterrestrials also have religion or have had spiritual experiences similar to ours. Similarly, these inquiries could lead to greater reflection and exploration of both existing and new religious and spiritual beliefs on our part as well as theirs. Without a doubt, the religious aspect would be one of the most crucial points, as many individuals might find coherence and harmony between these aspects, while others might perceive it as a source of tension and conflict. Remember that human beings have a need for belonging to a group and social acceptance. Hence, the belief in extraterrestrial life itself can provide a sense of community and belonging, especially when shared with like-minded individuals. Naturally, social acceptance and the desire to fit in can influence the adoption and maintenance of these thoughts. Therefore, once the fact of their existence is revealed or confirmed, we might face a clear social division between those in favor and those against.

Secondly, it's worth highlighting that popular culture and the media play a decisive role in shaping our beliefs. The portrayal of extraterrestrials in movies, TV shows, and books can mold our perception and generate greater acceptance or rejection of the idea of what the existence of extraterrestrial life is or could mean. This would be another significant focal point where governments might have acted or might act intentionally to shape human thought regarding their actual existence, a topic I will address in the next chapter.

However, in my opinion, there exists a third aspect. I'm referring to cognitive biases, such as confirmation bias and the tendency to seek patterns in ambiguous information, that could lead individuals to interpret inexplicable phenomena as evidence of extraterrestrial life. These biases can influence how we process information and lead us to find coincidences where there may be none. For example, we can discuss the phenomenon of pareidolia, suggestibility, and the false memory hypothesis.

The phenomenon of pareidolia is based on the human brain's tendency to perceive meaningful patterns, like recognizable faces or shapes, in ambiguous or random stimuli such as images, sounds, or textures. In other words, it's the mind's natural inclination to seek and find familiar shapes in stimuli that may lack intentional structure or design. This phenomenon is particularly noticeable when interpreting shapes or figures in everyday objects, like clouds resembling animals, faces in objects, burnt toast, or even detecting figures in surface features such as walls or floors, seeing faces in the Moon or rock formations, finding faces in damp stains on a wall, perceiving a face in inanimate objects like vehicles or buildings, and more. In essence, it's an example of how the human brain actively seeks patterns and meaning in the environment, even when those patterns aren't truly present, to attribute significance to our surroundings and make it somehow familiar. However, it can also lead to misconceptions or perceiving connections that don't actually exist. For this reason, in the context of searching for extraterrestrial life, pareidolia can lead to misinterpretations of images or data, resulting in a belief in the detection of extraterrestrial objects or beings in images or data that are simply the outcome of random patterns or visual artifacts.

When discussing suggestibility, we refer to the influence of one's own beliefs and expectations, which play a crucial role in how we interpret and remember events. This can cause some individuals to interpret ambiguous or unclear situations as interactions with extraterrestrial beings. Imagine a person who already firmly holds the belief in the existence of extraterrestrial life. This pre-existing belief acts as a filter through which they perceive the world around them. When such a person encounters an ambiguous or unclear situation, such as observing strange lights in the sky or seeing patterns in a rock formation, their mind tends to automatically adjust those perceptions to align with their expectations. Entrenched beliefs and expectations become unconscious suggestions that influence how they interpret and recall events. Therefore, these individuals are more likely to fill information gaps with details that align with their preconceived convictions. This can lead to the "enrichment" of experiences in subsequent narration, as suggestive details get integrated into memory coherently with pre-existing beliefs. For instance, a suggestible person who has had an unexplainable visual experience in the sky might recall it as a close encounter with an extraterrestrial craft, incorporating characteristics typical of UFO iconography.

The human mind, though wonderfully complex, can sometimes be deceptive. In the false memory hypothesis, recollections can be shaped and transformed over time, especially when it comes to emotional or impactful events, causing memory to be influenced by the intensity of emotions and the uniqueness of the experience. Over time, memories can be susceptible to distortion and the incorporation of elements that weren't present originally. In the context of extraterrestrial encounters, this could result in the formation of detailed, vivid memories of interactions with alien beings that never occurred in reality. The inclusion of fantastical elements in memory can be involuntary and often unconscious, leading to the formation of a narrative that combines real information with distorted details. In conclusion, the false memory hypothesis prompts us to consider how our memories can be malleable and how they can be shaped by external influences and internal processes.

Now, these very cognitive biases could themselves serve as explanations (tools) for those who, up to this point, possess the determination or orders to conceal it.

Similarly, personal experiences of inexplicable or unexplained phenomena for the individual (those that cannot be explained by science or conventional understanding) might lead some people to resort to the extraterrestrial hypothesis as a way to fill that gap in their knowledge or lack of understanding. But be cautious, once again, we encounter the dilemma between what the individual has experienced or claims to have lived through (to them, it is real, as in many mental pathologies) and what is actually real. I'm referring to experiences of UFO sightings or close encounters that repeat over time and generations, leading to a transfer of popular and cultural information and its consequent psychological impact on those who receive it.

CHAPTER 6

The influence of film, literatura, media and social media

In the midst of the 21st century, no one can doubt the tremendous impact that media and social media are having on our culture and, consequently, on the construction of our understanding of the world. Likewise, art forms such as cinema and literature have gradually seeped into what we conceive of as extraterrestrial life over time. These media-driven images and descriptions could "color" our interpretations, leading us to view extraterrestrial encounters in coherence with these representations, whether they be negative or positive.

In fact, each of us has a clear and detailed mental image of something that is entirely unknown at first. These iconic and stereotypical images have shaped extraterrestrial beings into creatures with large heads, big black eyes, slender bodies, piloting futuristic spacecraft, and carrying out abductions with dire consequences for the abducted. These representations ingrained in the collective mind establish a framework from which we interpret potentially inexplicable experiences. As examples, consider the effect of the "Grey Face," where someone who has grown up watching films and TV shows depicting extraterrestrials with features like a "grey face," such as large eyes and pale skin, might be more inclined to interpret an ambiguous experience as an encounter with these iconic "grey" extraterrestrials, fitting their narrative.

In this way, we can turn our attention to cinematic films that depict aliens as violent and dangerous entities for humanity, such as Ridley Scott's "Alien" (1979), Jim and John Thomas's "Predator" (1987), Roland Emmerich's "Independence Day" (1996), Steven Spielberg's "War of the Worlds" (2005), Neill Blomkamp's "District 9" (2009), the Strause brothers' "Skyline" (2010), Jonathan Liebesman's "Battle: Los Angeles" (2011), or John Krasinski's "A Quiet Place" (2018).

Conversely, we've also seen movies where extraterrestrials are portrayed as peaceful and even amusing, like Steven Spielberg's "E.T. the Extra-Terrestrial" (1982), Robert Zemeckis's "Contact" (1997), Greg Mottola's "Paul" (2011), Scott Derrickson's "The Day the Earth Stood Still" (2008), or even in scenarios where they are good, bad, and share their daily lives with us, as seen in the well-known "Men in Black" series by Barry Sonnenfeld, with its first installment dating back to 1997.

Interestingly, there is a significantly greater number of films depicting extraterrestrials as dangerous and threatening to humanity compared to those portraying them as benevolent and friendly. This is because most science fiction movies tend to focus on the conflict and danger posed by encounters with extraterrestrial beings. Consequently, there is a wide array of movies exploring this theme, which often appeals to the audience due to the abundance and richness of visual effects. Movies portraying extraterrestrials as kind and friendly beings are rarer since they can be more challenging to develop in terms of plot and conflict.

When it comes to literature, we encounter the same duality, with extraterrestrials being depicted as dangerous in famous novels such as H.G. Wells's "The War of the Worlds" (1898), Joe Haldeman's "The Forever War" (1974), Larry Niven's "Footfall" (1985), or S.K. Dunstall's "The Linesman" (2003).

In contrast, the friendly or benevolent beings take center stage in works like Isaac Asimov's "The Last Question" (1956), Frederik Pohl's "Gateway" (1977), Carl Sagan's "Contact" (1985), or David

Gerrold's "Encounter at Farpoint" (1987), among many others.

Likewise, in science fiction literature, there is also a greater number of works that present extraterrestrials as dangerous and menacing beings compared to those that portray them as benevolent and friendly. This tendency is attributed to the fact that conflicts and tensions arising from hostile encounters with extraterrestrials often provide more exciting and action-packed plots.

As a reader, you might have arrived at the same conclusion as I have—due to this cultural factor, we are predisposed to a negative concept of these beings. Consequently, the emotions that emerge with the announcement of the confirmation of extraterrestrial life are likely to lean towards fear and uncertainty.

Regarding the response of Instagrammers, TikTokers, and media outlets to the official communication of the existence of extraterrestrial life, it could vary and reflect the diversity of opinions and approaches in today's society. Naturally, it will depend on the personality and approach of each content creator, as well as how the news is presented and discussed in the media. There will likely be a mix of enthusiasm, skepticism, scientific interest, and online creativity. However, considering the principle of generating economic benefits through content views, I'm afraid that, as we have seen in examples from literature and cinema, the content is likely to be more dramatic, catastrophic, and apocalyptic, as this genre tends to attract more attention. This phenomenon could even precipitate certain actions by some individuals that initiate a conflict, leading to the effect of a self-fulfilling prophecy.

CHAPTER 7

Preparation for discovery

Preparing the population for the official announcement of extraterrestrial life is a delicate process that requires extremely careful consideration of various factors, including the impact on society, culture, and global population stability to avoid chaos. This process could be divided into the following phases:

Phase 1: Research and Assessment

First and foremost, a multidisciplinary task force should be established. Bringing together scientists, psychologists, sociologists, communicators, and religious leaders who can advise on the most complex process in human history. A thorough review of scientific evidence regarding the existence of extraterrestrial life should be conducted, and the possibility of communicating with them should be evaluated. As we are aware, some existing institutions include the SETI Institute (Search for Extraterrestrial Intelligence), the Breakthrough Listen program, the Mars Society, various NASA projects, projects of the International Organization of Planetary Sciences and Associated Sciences (IOPW), and projects from the European Southern Observatory (ESO), among many others.

Phase 2: Preparation of the Scientific and Religious Communities

Secondly, the gathered information and evidence should be communicated to the scientific community to secure their support and ensure they are ready to address questions and challenges. Similarly, religious leaders should be informed to discuss potential theological implications and help prepare their congregations. Interestingly, some religious leaders, in a personal capacity, have already addressed the issue of possible extraterrestrial life. In 1952, Pope Pius XII mentioned the possibility of other rational beings in the universe in an address to the Pontifical Academy of Sciences. He suggested that if they existed, they would be "our brothers" and that God would have created intelligent beings on other worlds. On various occasions, Pope Francis has spoken about the search for extraterrestrial life. In 2014, during a homily, he suggested that if extraterrestrials came to Earth, we would be willing to receive them as "our brothers" and evangelize them. In 2017, in a video message to astronauts on the International Space Station, Pope Francis discussed the importance of scientific collaboration to better understand God's Creation. Moreover, Brother Guy Consolmagno, director of the Vatican Observatory and Jesuit astronomer, has extensively spoken about the relationship between faith and science, including the possibility of extraterrestrial life. He emphasized that the existence of life on other planets does not contradict Catholic faith and that, as a scientist and believer, he sees the pursuit of truth in both fields. According to Consolmagno, "We already have parts of the Bible that say we are not the only intelligent things made by God." He clarified that "religion never wanted to say humans were the center of the universe. That's a misunderstanding of the old cosmology."

Phase 3: Public Communication Planning

Thirdly, a communication strategy should be developed by experts with a clear and careful approach. Explaining the scientific evidence in an accessible and understandable manner would be crucial. This scientific evidence supporting the existence of extraterrestrial life should reflect the methods and technologies used to collect data and how this data has been analyzed and verified. The importance of this discovery in the context of the search for life in the universe should be highlighted, discussing how this finding could broaden our understanding of biology and astrobiology. Finally, the focus should be on how the confirmation of extraterrestrial life could influence our perception of Earth's place in the cosmos and foster a broader perspective on life and diversity in the universe. In late July 2023, NASA Director Bill Nelson announced that due to the information generated about possible UFOs and "aliens," a group of scientists would prepare a report after thorough investigation into potential extraterrestrial life, making it public in August of the same year.

Phase 4: Preparing the Population in Advance

Fourthly, and depending on the timeline, a preliminary educational campaign should be conducted, gradually advancing the news. The objective would be to cultivate a positive cognitive predisposition among the majority of the Earth's population towards this new reality. This could be achieved by implementing a series of measures that younger generations would naturally absorb. Some of these measures could include: detachment from institutions or religious beliefs through discrediting campaigns or promoting the emergence of other trends with more positive characteristics; campaigns promoting awareness and respect for diversity in all its forms; legislation favoring the equal rights of other known animal species to those of humans; communication about discoveries of new terrestrial species previously unknown, potentially dangerous to humans, including viruses or bacteria; raising awareness and preparation regarding the limitation or possible absence of certain terrestrial resources or human freedoms that were previously taken for granted; exposure to radical changes in people's lives or those that involve a transgression of traditional values and, especially, those that are globally recognized; dependence on and submission to government states due to either a lack of general education and independent thinking capabilities or a lack of basic resources for survival; normalization and acceptance of uncertainty as a natural state.

CHAPTER 8

Sociopolitical and economic aspects
following the announcement

The communication of the existence of extraterrestrial life would have a profound impact on various global sociopolitical and economic aspects. While it's difficult to predict all implications with precision, I believe there are some key aspects that could be affected.

In terms of sociopolitical aspects, there would be a need to confront a worldwide reevaluation of identity and religion. Most religious doctrines would need to make adjustments to fit or accommodate the new information alongside their previously established teachings, leading to intense debates and profound reflections. Reaching new conclusions that satisfy all followers wouldn't be an easy task.

Regarding foreign policy and diplomacy, international relations would need to rapidly change, with new diplomatic protocols and international agreements being established as nations consider how to interact with possible extraterrestrial life forms.

The initial questions governments would grapple with are: Do they represent a threat? And are we safe? These uncertainties would trigger numerous national security and defense protocols. Likewise, discussions with other nations would be required to plan cooperative defense strategies and increase resources for space surveillance with the sole aim of safeguarding Earth from potential threats.

One of the most logical consequences would be the necessity of creating a Global Unity and Cooperation Unit. The news could act as a catalyst for the formation of a single global government where humanity could collectively address the challenge of understanding and attempting to communicate with an extraterrestrial civilization, without division or dissenting voices.

Regarding economic aspects, regardless of the consequences generated by the aforementioned sociopolitical changes, governments would need to shift priorities for certain expenditures, allocating more resources to research, space exploration, and, inevitably, the military and arms sectors.

The technology industry could potentially generate new economic opportunities to establish means of communication with the new extraterrestrial life forms.

The exploration of other planets potentially harboring confirmed extraterrestrial life, or even interaction with these beings, could lead to the identification of valuable space resources, such as rare minerals, water, or unknown materials, all of which would undoubtedly have long-term economic implications.

Lastly, the news could boost interest in space tourism, potentially opening a new economic industry centered around space travel and unique experiences. In fact, at the time of writing this book, several companies are already working in the space tourism industry, offering non-astronaut individuals the chance to travel to space. Among them are companies founded by some of the wealthiest individuals on the planet, such as SpaceX (founded by Elon Musk), Blue Origin (founded by Jeff Bezos), and Virgin Galactic (founded by Richard Branson).

Ultimately, the communication of the existence of extraterrestrial life would have a profound and multifaceted impact on society, politics, and the economy. It would be a gradual adaptation process that would require cooperation and leadership on both national and international levels to address the challenges and opportunities that arise.

CHAPTER 9

Qualities and psychological profile of the President of a World Unified Government

Before delving into this chapter, I must clarify that when using masculine terms, I do so for reasons of linguistic brevity (to avoid constant gender repetition). Naturally, this position could be fulfilled by either a man or a woman. Thus, describing an ideal president to govern all countries in the world involves a combination of personal qualities, leadership skills, and psychological characteristics that enable effective and respectful management of global challenges. This would be an unprecedentedly complex task. Consider that even in any single country, the two candidates for any presidency typically have their population divided by 50%. Being a single ruler on a global level seems an impossible mission. Nonetheless, and in brief, the following basic principles would apply:

Empathy and International Understanding: This president should be highly empathetic and capable of understanding diverse cultures, perspectives, and needs worldwide. They should be able to put themselves in others' shoes and consider how their decisions will impact the globe, with billions of human lives at stake.

Emotional Intelligence: Emotional intelligence is crucial for handling international relations and diplomatic situations. This individual should control their own emotions, comprehend others' emotions, and use this understanding to build strong relationships.

Global Thinking and Long-Term Vision: A global leader should look beyond short-term issues and possess a strategic, long-term vision to address global challenges stemming from these new relationships between distinct species, while also addressing ongoing crucial matters like climate change, poverty, and current or future international conflicts.

Effective Communication Skills: The ability to communicate clearly and persuasively is pivotal for a global leader. They should convey their vision, listen to other leaders, and communicate with empathy and respect. In this case, non-verbal communication consistent with their speech and their natural expression forms would be crucial. Proficiency in the two or three most spoken languages in the world (English, Chinese, and Spanish) would also be advisable.

Tolerance and Respect for Diversity: This prospective ideal president should be tolerant and respectful towards all religions, cultures, ethnic groups, and even life forms in the universe. They would need to foster cooperation and understanding among diverse nations and communities.

Negotiation and Compromise Skills: The ability to negotiate and find compromise solutions would be essential for a singular global leader. They should be capable of resolving conflicts peacefully and working with leaders of different ideologies.

Resilience and Stress Tolerance: Global governance might be the most stressful and challenging political position ever. For this reason, resilience and the ability to manage stress and make tough decisions under pressure are crucial.

Charismatic and Inspirational Leadership: A global leader should have the capacity to inspire people and mobilize nations towards common goals. They need a natural charisma that attracts different cultures and builds trust.

Honesty and Ethics: Currently, these values are highly sought due to their sad absence in most current presidents. Hence, this person should be able to demonstrate an impeccable history, lifestyle, and conduct, free from any blemishes on their record, and be an example in terms of honesty, transparency, and ethical behavior.

Open-Mindedness and Adaptability: Given the ever-changing world, and the potential for rapid changes, this individual should not only possess an open mind but be willing and prepared to adapt to new circumstances and challenges.

It's important to note that no individual is perfect, although they should strive for these ideals. I acknowledge that these traits represent a simplified idealization. Moreover, this potential global leadership would involve complex ongoing interaction between leaders from different countries and cultures, making an ideal president to govern all countries in the world a facilitator of collaborative work to address common problems and build a harmonious united world.

CHAPTER 10

Psychological impact of disclosure

There is no doubt that the official communication of the existence of extraterrestrial life would have a series of severe psychological implications for humans. These implications would naturally vary based on individual beliefs, culture, and prior preparation of each person, but I will venture to mention some potential consequences below.

On one hand, confirming the existence of extraterrestrial life could alter our perception of humanity and our place in the universe. It might generate a sense of humility in acknowledging that we are not the only intelligent beings in the cosmos, leading to a reevaluation of our values, beliefs, and priorities. This fact necessitates the need to unlearn all that has been learned to date, comprehending the magnitude of this task given thousands of years of history.

Similarly, for a significant portion of the global population, the revelation of extraterrestrial life could challenge their traditional religious beliefs. The existence of beings from other planets would raise questions about the nature of God, creation, and humanity's relationship with the divine. This could trigger internal conflicts (reconciling the existence of extraterrestrial life with one's own prior teachings and beliefs) and tensions among different communities with established religious beliefs, potentially leading to serious conflicts among them. Additionally, it could challenge cultural and national identity. Values, beliefs, and narratives deeply rooted in a specific culture or nation could be questioned or reevaluated. This could generate internal (local) and external (with other countries) conflicts. A reevaluation of established systems of knowledge and authority would ensue, prompting questions about the validity of our scientific, political, and religious institutions in relation to understanding the universe. This could foster increased skepticism toward power structures and a quest for new approaches, paradigms, or even encourage anarchism and individualism. Conversely, it might be an opportunity for global unity, although that would entail embracing the possible creation of a new and singular world order.

More significantly, from my perspective, this revelation could challenge our understanding of reality at an individual level. Without a doubt, we would ask questions about the nature of life, evolution, and the boundaries of what we consider possible, and why not, ethical or moral. This could generate a sense of wonder, but also trigger doubts and confusion about what we thought we knew. A destabilization of our psyche, which not all individuals might be prepared for. When referring to emotional or psychological reactions, I mean astonishment, fear, concern, and anxiety. Consequently, numerous people might feel threatened or insecure even in the absence of real evidence, possibly giving rise to new, previously unknown phobias, negatively influencing psychological well-being and how we relate to ourselves and others. In general, it could lead to increased anxiety, stress, and widespread uncertainty. People might grapple with feelings of vulnerability and a sense of lack of control over the unknown. Hence, it would be necessary to provide psychological support and resources to help those affected manage these emotions and adapt to the changes. Therefore, an unprecedented deployment of mental health professionals would be necessary, likely unattainable in numerical terms with the current resources.

Nevertheless, we must consider that the impacts can be both positive and negative, depending on individual perspectives and specific circumstances. For this reason, we could also contemplate other possibilities, such as fascination and enthusiasm as a reaction that involves wanting to learn more about these unknown life forms. People experiencing this might feel more open and curious about the unknown and even develop a sense of connection and unity with other life forms in the universe, elevating them to a higher level. The idea that life is more abundant and diverse in the universe could also generate joy and hope, as it could be seen as an opportunity for humanity to come together around a shared goal, regardless of its nature. We could also speak of euphoria and optimism about potential opportunities for collaboration, knowledge exchange, and scientific advances that could arise from this discovery. Numerous scientists and space exploration enthusiasts might have increased motivation to continue researching and gaining understanding of extraterrestrial life.

However, we cannot forget about a group that, despite being a minority, might also exist. I'm referring to those who, initially, might react with skepticism or indifference until presented with more evidence or even witness or participate in an event that forms their opinion.

In conclusion, we would be facing a cascade of profound existential questions that, at a simplistic and individual level, would prompt reflection on the meaning of one's own existence in a broader and universal context. Taking the more positive and generalistic perspective, it could also promote the exploration of diversity and tolerance towards the different. Most likely, it would foster greater openness towards other life forms and the understanding that diversity extends beyond our planet, which could positively impact how we relate to different cultures and perspectives here on Earth.

CHAPTER 11

Psychological impacts of the UFO phenomenon

I couldn't overlook in the writing of this book the potential link between certain psychopathologies or psychological disorders and purported UFO sightings or experiences related to close encounters with extraterrestrial beings, such as abductions. While some individuals strongly believe in the authenticity of their experiences, accounts of alien abductions may involve elements that could also be explained by other phenomena, such as vivid dreams, hallucinations, sleep paralysis, and other psychological disorders.

However, it's important to highlight that not all individuals reporting these encounters necessarily have a psychopathology. In fact, I dare say that the majority of them had no pathology before these events, although the question will always remain whether the imagined event was the first symptom of the later diagnosed pathology, or if the real event was the logical trigger for such a pathology.

If we consider the first hypothesis, we could briefly and succinctly discuss the following disorders:

Schizotypal Personality Disorder

Schizotypal Personality Disorder is a personality disorder characterized by patterns of eccentric thinking, unconventional beliefs, and a peculiar way of relating to others. While it's important to emphasize that not all individuals reporting encounters with extraterrestrials have schizotypal personality disorder, some accounts may exhibit similarities with the characteristics of this disorder. Let's examine how these aspects relate:

Eccentric thinking and unconventional beliefs: Individuals with this disorder may be prone to embrace unconventional or mystical ideas that differ from mainstream beliefs. In the context of encounters with extraterrestrials, people reporting such experiences may sometimes have beliefs that challenge established social and scientific norms.

Unusual perceptual experiences: Likewise, they may experience unusual perceptions, such as perceptual illusions or depersonalization experiences. These experiences could contribute to the misinterpretation of everyday events as interactions with extraterrestrial beings.

Social relationship difficulties: They may also struggle with social relationships due to their peculiar communication style and focus on unconventional topics. This could also manifest in accounts of encounters with extraterrestrials where they feel misunderstood by others or have difficulties expressing their experiences.

Perception of hidden communications or secret meanings: People with this disorder may perceive hidden or secret meanings in seemingly ordinary situations. In this context, they might interpret coincidences or random events as signals of extraterrestrial communication.

Delusions or Hallucinations (Linked to Possible Schizophrenia)

These delusions or hallucinations could be related to some psychotic disorder, with the subsequent interpretation of experiences as both literal and real, yet extraordinary. What might appear as a genuine and convincing experience to them may not have an objective basis in reality. It's important to consider that psychotic symptoms can color and distort perception, affecting how individuals experience and recall events. Typically, the predominant psychotic disorder in these cases would be schizophrenia.

Delusions are false, unfounded, and unchanging beliefs that are not shared by others in the same cultural context. In the context we're discussing, individuals might develop delusions that they are being watched, contacted, or manipulated by beings from other worlds. These delusions can be persistent and resistant to correction, reflecting the characteristic nature of delusions.

On the other hand, hallucinations are sensory perceptions without an actual external stimulus. Auditory and visual hallucinations are the most common and can contribute to the experience of encounters with extraterrestrials. Individuals might report hearing extraterrestrial voices or seeing spaceships and alien beings that others neither see nor perceive.

Stress Factors and Dissociative Disorder

These factors can influence how we perceive, interpret, and remember experiences. In the context of encounters with extraterrestrial beings, these factors can play a significant role in shaping accounts that appear related to life beyond Earth.

Extreme stress situations can profoundly impact a person's psychology. Stress can trigger intense physiological and emotional responses, influencing perception and information processing. In high emotional tension situations, people might be more prone to interpret events in a distorted manner or give them a meaning that reflects their fears, anxieties, or personal beliefs, which in this case would be related to the phenomenon discussed in this book.

Dissociation is a psychological defense mechanism in which a person disconnects from their thoughts, emotions, sensations, or even their sense of identity. It can manifest as a feeling of being "out of oneself" or as if one is observing from outside oneself. In extreme stress situations, some individuals might experience dissociation as a way to escape emotional distress. These sensations can subsequently be consciously interpreted as a potential alien abduction.

Experiences of extreme stress and dissociation could also be related to acute stress disorder, post-traumatic stress disorder (PTSD), and dissociative identity disorder. In these cases, individuals might experience momentary dissociation that is interpreted as a real encounter with extraterrestrial beings. As is often the case in these situations, this interpretation is influenced by cultural, social, or personal factors, hence the content of the interpretation. As a result, they might vividly and elaborately recount these encounters with extraterrestrial beings, sincerely believing in the reality of these experiences. These accounts can be emotionally intense and coherent within the framework of dissociation.

If we turn to the second hypothesis and assume the truth of the event, we could say that the pathologies or disorders would be different.

Post-Traumatic Stress Disorder (PTSD)

PTSD is a psychological response to traumatic events that can have a lasting impact on a person's mental health. In these cases, we would find the presence of intrusive memories and re-experiencing of traumatic events. Those who claim to have had close encounters with extraterrestrials might repeatedly relive the details of the encounter in the form of memories, images, or unwanted thoughts. These intrusive memories can cause significant distress and logically affect their quality of life. Similarly, they might experience recurring nightmares related to the event. These dreams would be highly detailed, similar in content, and distressing, potentially reliving the experience and increasing anxiety. This, in turn, would result in a higher likelihood of severe anxiety and startle responses, feeling highly tense in situations reminding them of the extraterrestrial encounter. Sounds, smells, or places associated with the experience could trigger intense anxiety and fear responses. Individuals who have reported alien abductions often experienced the situation as threatening and beyond their control, feeling much more vulnerable, which further contributes to the development of more PTSD symptoms. Consequently, all these symptoms would significantly affect their quality of life. Emotional, cognitive, and behavioral difficulties would typically interfere with interpersonal relationships, work functioning, and overall health.

Panic Disorder

Panic disorder is an anxiety disorder characterized by recurrent and intense episodes of sudden fear accompanied by physical and cognitive symptoms. Panic disorder episodes often include symptoms such as rapid or strong palpitations, excessive sweating, tremors, shortness of breath, dizziness, nausea, and an overwhelming feeling of fear or loss of control. These symptoms can be extremely intense and may be triggered by situations perceived as threatening or dangerous. Individuals experiencing close encounters with extraterrestrial beings or UFO sightings might experience intense anxiety during or after the experience. Unusual or inexplicable events like these can provoke significant anxiety responses in some individuals, especially if they feel they have no control over the situation or if they interpret the experience as threatening. In some cases, the anxiety cycle can perpetuate itself. An individual who has experienced a panic disorder episode related to this topic might develop heightened apprehension toward similar situations or even anticipate future encounters. This anxious anticipation, in turn, could increase the likelihood of experiencing more panic disorder episodes in the future.

It's important to note that this type of mental disorder can be treated with therapy and, in some cases, medication. Individuals experiencing these disorders should seek professional help to address their symptoms and understand how anxiety can influence their future experiences, thereby breaking the cycle.

Generalized Anxiety Disorder (GAD)

Generalized Anxiety Disorder (GAD) is an anxiety disorder characterized by excessive and persistent worry about various aspects of life, often related to future events, health, family, work, and more. In the context we are discussing, we would refer to constant, uncontrollable, excessive, and anticipatory worry about possible future and new encounters with extraterrestrial beings and everything related to the unknown. This anxious anticipation could lead to a constant state of alertness and rumination about how to handle such a situation. Associated symptoms would include physical symptoms like muscle tension, fatigue, sleep difficulties, and emotional symptoms like irritability and difficulty concentrating. These symptoms might intensify when the worry is focused on hypothetical events. In this way, GAD would interfere with a person's daily functioning, affecting their ability to fulfill work, social, and familial responsibilities and impeding normal activities. Similar to other anxiety disorders, the anxiety cycle of GAD can be self-perpetuating, emphasizing the importance of efforts to break that cycle through seeking professional help.

Somatization Disorder

Somatization Disorder, also known as Somatic Symptom Disorder, is a disorder in which individuals experience unexplained physical symptoms or health issues that lack a clear medical cause. In this context, they might experience a wide range of symptoms like body pains, extreme fatigue, gastrointestinal problems, and similar issues. Numerous cases have been reported where subjects claim to have been sexually abused as part of experimentation or exploration of their genitals for reproductive studies or even the insertion of foreign objects like chips into different parts of their bodies. These localized symptoms could emerge as a response to anxiety, stress, or intense emotions related to the experience, as the mind and body are tightly interconnected, and emotional responses can manifest as physical symptoms. We must also consider the nocebo effect, or the negative influence that expectations and beliefs can have on health. If someone believes they have been exposed to something harmful, even if there's no real medical cause, they can develop somatic symptoms in response to that belief. In the case of these encounters, if someone believes they've had a potentially harmful experience in certain parts of their body, they could develop highly localized somatic symptoms as a result.

Likewise, these somatic symptoms should undergo proper medical evaluation to rule out physical causes. If no medical cause is found, then psychological and emotional factors should be considered and addressed.

As I have previously mentioned in this book, it's important to note that reports of UFO sightings and encounters with extraterrestrial beings can also have non-pathological explanations, such as misinterpretations of natural phenomena, suggestibility, lighting and shadow effects, among others. Each case must be evaluated individually, and in some cases, it might be appropriate to consider psychological factors alongside external factors to fully understand the reported experience.

CHAPTER 12

The first case of extraterrestrial abduction and preceding psychological studies

Considering various literature sources, there are numerous accounts of alien abductions, although it is true that most of these experiences do not seem to possess solid scientific evidence and therefore are difficult to objectively verify. Nevertheless, when we speak of scientific evidence, we must bear in mind that the terms of this science have been defined by ourselves, with the consequent limitations that this fact may entail, thus necessitating leaving a door open to other types of parameters, thereby relativizing any conclusion.

Over the years, cases of alien abductions have emerged that have captured public attention and have been discussed in literature and media. To avoid delving into this point, I will limit myself to citing the first reported case.

The Case of Betty and Barney Hill (1961): Betty and Barney Hill claimed to have been abducted by extraterrestrials in 1961 and subjected to medical examinations aboard a spacecraft. Their case was one of the first to receive extensive media coverage and has been widely discussed in the ufology community. Below, I quote the article that journalist Elena Mengual wrote for El Mundo newspaper on October 22, 2004: "It was September 19, 1961. Betty and her husband, Barney, were returning to Portsmouth after a vacation in Canada, where they had traveled in search of some respite to alleviate Barney's ulcer, perhaps a consequence of the enormous social pressure they faced during a time when interracial marriages were not well regarded. According to their account, as they were driving through the White Mountains of New Hampshire late at night, they saw a light in the sky that they initially mistook for a star. When they realized it was following them, Barney stopped the car to grab his binoculars and, incidentally, his revolver. He looked toward the glow and observed colorful lights and windows, and through them, silhouettes. Very frightened, he returned to the vehicle and sped away. However, they arrived home with stained and torn clothing and a two-hour delay. Two hours that remained a blank in their memory. The two years following the incident were a nightmare for the Hills: Barney's ulcer worsened, and both suffered anxiety attacks, hypertension, insomnia, and nightmares. Nightmares in which they were abducted by strange beings. Plagued by these disorders, they turned to a prestigious psychiatrist and neurologist from Boston, Benjamin Simon, a specialist in hypnotherapy. The doctor separately subjected them to sessions of regressive hypnosis, in which the couple 'reconstructed' the two-hour memory gap: according to their account, they had been abducted by extraterrestrials and subjected to various physical tests aboard a spaceship. The aliens allegedly then programmed Betty and Barney's minds so they couldn't remember what had happened and released them. According to the couple's description, the extraterrestrials were beings about 1.5 meters tall, bald, with grayish skin, pear-shaped heads, large cat-like eyes, small noses and mouths, and communicated via telepathy, although the group leader also spoke English. A star map was even drawn based on Betty's descriptions, which were, according to her, derived from the teachings of the extraterrestrial 'leader.' In due course, the existence of two stars featured on that map would be verified. The military would also confirm that on that night, the radar at Pease Air Force Base had detected an unidentified object, though it had "no consequences," according to the military report. Dr. Simon did not believe his patients' version - who from that moment onwards became regulars on radio and television shows - and claimed that people do not always tell the truth under hypnosis. For him, the

Hills suffered from amnesia, and Betty used her extraterrestrial dreams to fill in that gap in memory, which she transferred to her husband's subconscious by recounting her nightmares. However, it was never clear why they suffered from amnesia.

When I refer to scientific research on extraterrestrial encounters from a psychological perspective, I must say that it is a relatively small and controversial field. Some studies have attempted to analyze and understand the experiences of those who claim to have had this type of encounter with extraterrestrial beings. Below, I present a summary of some of these studies, inviting the reader to explore them:

"Close Encounters of the Fourth Kind: Alien Abduction and the Medical Professional" (1988) by John Mack: John Mack, a psychiatrist and professor at Harvard University, conducted a study on people who claimed to have had extraterrestrial encounters. Although criticized by some in the scientific community, Mack argued that his findings supported the possibility that these experiences were real for the individuals.

"Unusual Personal Experiences: An Analysis of the Data from Three National Surveys Conducted by the Roper Organization" (1991) by Roper Poll: This survey focused on "unusual" experiences reported by respondents, including UFO sightings and encounters with extraterrestrials. The results suggested that a small percentage of the population had experienced such events.

"The Myth of Alien Abduction" (1994) by Susan Clancy: Susan Clancy, a psychologist, examined claims of alien abduction from a skeptical perspective. She argued that many of these experiences could be explained by psychological and social factors, such as suggestion and sleep paralysis.

"Experiencers of UFO Phenomena: A Descriptive Survey of Persons Reporting Contact with UFOs/Extraterrestrials" (1992) by Leo Sprinkle and Craig R. Lundahl: This study surveyed individuals who claimed to have had encounters with extraterrestrial beings. The results showed that many participants had childhood histories involving paranormal phenomena and extraterrestrial experiences.

"The Role of Personality in UFO Witness and Abduction Claims: A Four Factor Study of Personality Structure and Fantasy Proneness in the UFO Witness and Abductee Population" (1997) by Michael Thalbourne and Lance Storm: This study investigated the relationship between personality and claims of UFO sightings and extraterrestrial abductions. The results suggested that certain personality traits and high levels of fantasy proneness might be associated with such claims.

"Alleged Alien Abduction: A Retrospective Study of Twelve Cases" (1998) by Etzel Cardeña, Steven Jay Lynn, and Stanley Krippner: This study retrospectively examined twelve cases of individuals claiming to have been abducted by extraterrestrials. The researchers found that participants often had histories of intense dream experiences and altered states of consciousness.

As mentioned earlier, the characteristics and casuistry of each experience can vary, while also sharing common elements. For this reason, some scientists suggest that some of these experiences could be attributed to factors such as suggestion, sleep paralysis, pronounced fantasy, and other psychological and sociocultural factors.

CHAPTER 13

Therapeutic approach to experiences of encounters with extraterrestrial beings

Experiences of encounters with extraterrestrial beings, whether real or imagined by individuals, constitute a complex psychological phenomenon that can have a profound and significant impact on people's lives. In such cases, mental health professionals can play a crucial role by providing a safe space to explore and understand these experiences, as well as offering support and tools to manage the associated emotional reactions. In this chapter, I will summarize how therapists could address these experiences from a compassionate and evidence-based perspective.

Establishing a Trusting Environment: The initial step in therapy is to create an atmosphere of trust and acceptance. Just like with any other case, therapists should demonstrate empathy and openness so that patients feel comfortable sharing their experiences, even if they may appear unusual or hard to comprehend.

Validation and Normalization: Therapists should validate patients' experiences and normalize their emotional reactions. Acknowledging that these experiences are real for the individual, regardless of how they might be interpreted externally, helps reduce stigma and shame.

Exploration of Beliefs and Meanings: Professionals can assist patients in exploring their beliefs and meanings surrounding encounters with extraterrestrial beings. This could involve investigating how these experiences integrate into their belief system and how they impact their daily life. This point, as seen in previous chapters of this book, can be extremely influential.

Emotional Management Tools: Providing emotional regulation strategies is essential. Therapists should teach techniques such as mindfulness and relaxation to help patients cope with potential symptoms like anxiety, fear, or confusion associated with these experiences.

Psychoeducation about Paranormal Experiences: Offering evidence-based information about paranormal phenomena and psychological explanations can help patients understand their experiences from a scientific perspective, thereby reducing distress.

Exploration of Underlying Factors: Therapists can explore underlying factors that might contribute to experiences of extraterrestrial encounters, such as stress, past traumas, or medical conditions. Identifying and addressing these areas can help contextualize the experiences and resolve generated conflicts.

Focus on Resilience and Strengths: Assisting clients in recognizing their strengths and coping abilities can empower them to manage emotional reactions to any type of psychological issue or conflict that arises in our lives. Highlighting their resilience can provide them with a greater sense of control.

Cognitive Restructuring Therapy: In some cases, therapists can employ cognitive restructuring techniques to challenge negative or distorted beliefs related to encounters with extraterrestrial beings and promote more adaptive thinking.

Integration into Identity and Personal Meaning: Helping patients explore how these experiences impact their sense of identity and understanding of the world can be a transformative process. Therapy can aid in integrating these experiences into their personal narrative in a way that holds positive meaning.

Collaborative and Multidisciplinary Work: Therapists handling such cases should collaborate with other professionals, such as medical doctors, to ensure that all physical and emotional aspects of these experiences are addressed. This would ensure a comprehensive approach to the client's well-being and rule out other possible associated pathologies.

Ultimately, the goal of such therapies would be to provide a safe and supportive space where patients can explore, process, and understand their experiences of encounters with extraterrestrial beings in a way that allows them to confront the emotional impact and find a greater sense of balance and well-being in their lives.

CHAPTER 14

How should we psychologically prepare for accepting the existence of extraterrestrial life?

As in many aspects of life, the theoretical and practical knowledge acquired prior to experiencing an event that could have a strong psychological impact is crucial.

Unfortunately, we are facing an event that lacks such resources, which is one of the personal motivations that led me to write this book.

Because of this, I would divide it into two parts. The first part would focus on preparation as a form of prevention, and the second part would address action as a form of reaction.

Regarding prevention, I would advocate for a greater need for education and dissemination concerning this event. Effective psychological preparation would involve educating society about the possibility of extraterrestrial life over time. This could be achieved through educational campaigns, television programs, documentaries, and scientific talks providing information about space exploration, astrobiology, and research into extraterrestrial life. Gradual familiarization with the topic can help reduce the sudden emotional impact of the news. For this reason, communication and psychology experts could play a crucial role in managing societal expectations. It's important to emphasize that the discovery of extraterrestrial life does not necessarily entail the arrival of alien beings on Earth. Clarifying the boundaries of what has been discovered can prevent misunderstandings and unfounded fears. If we look at the latest news being published in the media, this plan might already be in progress. Let's hope and trust that we have sufficient time for this.

Continuing with the educational aspect, promoting an open and adaptable mindset would be essential. Society can be encouraged to consider the possibility of extraterrestrial life as an opportunity to expand our understanding of the universe and our place within it. Adapting to new realities can be smoother when curiosity, diversity in all forms, the possibility of shared understanding spaces, and the pursuit of greater knowledge that brings global benefits are embraced. This is where international collaboration and dialogue among all countries worldwide should begin, contributing to a greater sense of community and unity during a time of change. Sharing perspectives, knowledge, and experiences among different cultures and nations can help mitigate isolation or fear. Being in situations of armed conflicts and polarization in extreme political ideologies only leads to greater distance, less unity, and therefore more vulnerability.

Lastly, I would begin establishing a global network of professionals who could provide psychological, emotional, and spiritual support for those individuals who may experience identity crises or exacerbation of their pathologies as a result of the news. In my humble opinion, the involvement of religious and spiritual leaders would be fundamental in aiding those who find themselves reconciling their beliefs with the newfound knowledge of extraterrestrial life.

In a more reactive second phase, or put differently, once this unique and potentially disruptive news has been released, I would advise individuals to:

Focus on the Positives. Undoubtedly, there are exciting and positive aspects to the discovery. We have the opportunity to be (presumably) the first generation of human beings that can learn more about the diversity of the universe, spiritually and cognitively grow to a much higher level, and benefit from possible technological and scientific advances in an exponential manner. It could be a great opportunity for you, as an individual, to join a learning group or become an expert in a subject you've always wanted to know more about, and which might help you better understand various scientific aspects of this event. Consider that you could positively contribute to society's adaptation to the news, which could also empower you.

Maintain an Open Mind. Approach the news with a curious attitude and recognize that the existence of extraterrestrial life doesn't necessarily change your values, beliefs, or identity. Visualize it as simply adding a new ingredient, something that can enhance rather than diminish.

Seek Reliable Information from Scientific and Authorized Sources. There will likely be numerous individuals (Instagrammers, TikTokers, or whichever application is trending) and alarmist and catastrophic media outlets seeking to generate economic revenue through visits to their platforms, regardless of the psychological consequences their content may provoke in their followers. Strive to obtain objective information and draw your own conclusions.

Validate Your Emotions. It's normal to feel a range of emotions such as awe, uncertainty, or even fear, as previously described. Therefore, allow time for your feelings to evolve. Create an emergency action plan that makes you feel more secure. In this case, having established meeting points with family members in case communications fail, or identifying refuge locations stocked with food, water, and medicine, can provide the security of fulfilling the most basic physiological needs on Maslow's hierarchy.

Talk About Your Feelings. Share your thoughts and emotions with friends, family, or mental health professionals. Dialogue can help you process your reactions and gain different perspectives. Reflect on how this discovery might influence your understanding of life, the universe, and your place within it. Seek new meanings and purposes in your life and share them with your loved ones. Similarly, if you hold strong religious beliefs, seek guidance from religious or spiritual leaders who can help you integrate the news with your faith.

Find a Balance Between Staying Informed and Disconnecting When Needed. Allowing yourself time to process information and then disconnecting will prevent emotional overload.

Connect with Nature. If possible, spend time outdoors and receive the necessary sunlight to synthesize vitamin D and improve your mood. Additionally, it can help you feel more grounded to your origins and identity as a human being and earthling by definition, as you assimilate the news.

Lastly, remember that each person may have a unique experience when facing this news. Giving yourself permission to process your emotions and seeking the support you need is crucial for healthy adaptation. If you feel fear or anxiety, identify underlying causes and work on gradually addressing them. Cognitive-behavioral therapy can be helpful for addressing irrational fear. Turning to the network of professionals that has been established could be the best option. In the case of being confined to homes, we have the previous experience of the Covid-19 pandemic in 2020, so curiously, we would already have knowledge of the previous experience as well as various resources to turn to.

CHAPTER 15

Psychology of communication with extraterrestrial beings

The psychology of communication is a branch of social psychology that focuses on understanding how individuals perceive, interpret, process, and transmit information in the process of sharing ideas. Similarly, it examines how psychological factors influence how people communicate with each other, whether verbally, nonverbally, or through various forms of media.

The psychology of communication encompasses a variety of areas and concepts, such as:

Perception and Attention: Studies how individuals select and process information from their environment, and how these processes influence the interpretation of communicative messages.

Social Interaction: Examines how social relationships, cultural norms, and group dynamics affect how people communicate and interact with one another.

Verbal and Nonverbal Communication: Analyzes both spoken language and nonverbal aspects like facial expressions, gestures, postures, and other nonverbal cues that influence communication and message interpretation.

Cognition and Understanding: Investigates how individuals process and understand information, as well as how they construct meaning from the messages they receive.

Technology-Mediated Communication: Explores how digital platforms and information technology influence how people communicate and relate in the digital environment.

Persuasive Communication: Analyzes the use of persuasion strategies in communication to influence others' attitudes, beliefs, and behaviors.

Intercultural Communication: Focuses on how cultural and linguistic differences impact communication between individuals from different backgrounds and cultural contexts.

Communication in Conflict Situations: Studies how conflicts are managed and resolved through communication, and how psychological factors can influence the dynamics of such conflicts.

Communication in Therapy and Counseling Contexts: Examines how mental health professionals communicate with their clients to provide emotional support and address psychological issues.

However, of course, we should consider an event unprecedented in human history, such as the first contact with an extraterrestrial species. Effective communication would be essential to establish a solid foundation of understanding and prevent misunderstandings that could lead to conflict with dire consequences. Below, I venture to suggest some techniques that could be employed in this hypothetical first contact:

Visual and Symbolic Communication: We should use images, symbols, icons, and visual representations that can transcend the barriers of verbal language. Diagrams, charts, and visual representations of mathematical and scientific concepts could also be useful for conveying precise information to civilizations more advanced than ours. In this case, mathematics and sciences are considered a universal language. Concepts like numbers, physical constants, and mathematical formulas might be understood by intelligent beings from anywhere in the universe, though, once again, this is based on a very human assumption. Similarly, using physical objects or three-dimensional geometric representations could aid in communicating abstract and complex concepts.

Music and Sounds: Music and sounds could be used to establish an emotional and cultural connection. Rhythmic patterns and simple melodies could convey emotions and moods. Considering that loud or deep noises alert and scare animals, perceiving them as danger, we should avoid them. Similarly, we should exercise caution with their frequencies, as miscalculations in their auditory levels could be interpreted as an attack.

Digital and Binary Language: Transmitting digital signals in binary code could be an efficient way to convey information, as it is a fundamental basis of modern technology and communication.

Light and Color Patterns: Using light and color patterns could be a way to transmit information in visual forms that could be detected and recognized by advanced technology or even biological perceptions. As with sounds, extreme caution should be exercised regarding their intensity, as some animal species are blinded by certain levels of luminance.

Communication Across Time: Using sequences or patterns that reflect astronomical phenomena, such as the positions of planets or stars at a specific moment, could serve as a way to establish a temporal frame of reference. It might be a first step towards something that should be familiar and thus interpreted positively.

Establishing Patterns and Repetitions: Using patterns and repetitions in transmissions could help extraterrestrial beings identify intent behind communication and recognize significant elements in sequences that could not occur randomly or by chance.

Establishing Cultural Contexts: One of the key points would be observing signs or symbols that might appear on their spacecraft, possible objects, or even on their bodies to attempt to identify distinctly extraterrestrial cultural elements and thereby try to understand their meaning, providing us with a context that could facilitate communication.

Lastly, it's important to begin with basic information and gradually advance to more complex concepts in order to allow for progressive adaptation and understanding on both sides. Let's remember that when we approach any known animal species, we do so slowly and gradually to show non-invasiveness.

It's important to remember that, in a first contact scenario, caution and patience would be crucial. Establishing protocols and working with experts in linguistics, intercultural communication, and other disciplines like communication with diverse animal species would be necessary to ensure that communication is as precise and understandable as possible.

CHAPTER 16

The danger of chaos in the face of the news and how to avoid it

A news of such magnitude could naturally lead to social chaos or even be exploited by criminals as an excuse to create a situation that would favor their own criminal interests. We can anticipate a real risk that, especially in major cities, panic could spread, leading to circumstances or characteristics akin to a wartime scenario, accompanied by the emergence of crimes and violent acts stemming from the breakdown of social order and lack of control. These crimes may vary in severity and nature, and could include:

Robberies and Looting: The absence of law enforcement and the presence of authorities could result in an increase in robberies and looting of stores, homes, and businesses. Criminals could take advantage of the opportunity to unlawfully acquire valuable goods and resources.

Interpersonal Violence: Chaos and insecurity can give rise to fights, assaults, and homicides. Personal conflicts and tensions could escalate in a situation of war and disorder, as regrettably seen in countries that have experienced civil wars in the past.

Drug and Arms Trafficking: Criminal organizations could exploit the power vacuum to intensify drug and arms trafficking, contributing to insecurity and exacerbating the situation. The price of weapons might exponentially increase in value, being seen as resources for personal defense and necessities.

Extortion and Blackmail: Similarly, this panic-inducing situation of facing an unknown enemy could be exploited by criminal organizations to extort and blackmail individuals of high purchasing power, vulnerable businesses, government officials, even weak governments, demanding money or other resources in exchange for protection or security.

Sexual and Gender-based Violence: Unfortunately, during the outbreak of social crises, incidents of sexual and gender-based violence tend to rise, including rapes, abuses, harassment, and even abductions of minors for human trafficking or organ trade. In such cases, human rights can be broadly violated, including arbitrary detentions, torture, and summary executions.

Cybercrimes: Disorganization and disruption of public services would facilitate cybercrimes, such as personal information theft and online fraud.

It's important to bear in mind that such situations would be highly unfavorable and devastating not only for urban inhabitants but for society as a whole, and in this case, for the human race, weakening us against a possible enemy that might not even be so.

But if, despite all efforts by armed forces and competent governments, social chaos were to erupt in your city, prioritizing the safety and well-being of your family is fundamental. Though it's impossible to predict events exactly, here are some general steps that could help you take measures to protect your family. I couldn't miss the opportunity to mention them.

As with everything in life, proactive planning tends to be a good strategy. Establish a meeting point that all your family members know and set a timeframe (for example, 24 hours) to meet there in case phone lines and the internet are down. Design an evacuation plan that includes safe escape routes to reach the meeting point and another to leave there for a place you consider safer (away from large urban centers). In the place you've deemed safer, try to have stored or make sure there are non-perishable food items, drinkable water, medications, and basic supplies as access to these resources will likely be limited. Prepare one or several emergency backpacks ready with essential items like a first aid kit, dynamo-powered flashlights, solar chargers to power specific devices, important documents, and warm clothing.

If you couldn't have any of this prepared or have to remain within an urban center, stay away from the most conflict-prone or dangerous areas (streets or shopping centers) and follow the guidance of local authorities. Strengthen home security with additional locks, fortified doors and windows, and even alarm systems if possible. If you have to move through the streets, keep a low profile, avoid unnecessary attention to prevent becoming a victim of criminal acts or conflicts. Establish relationships and connections with neighbors and community members for mutual support and to stay informed about the situation's developments. Stay informed about news and developments in the area through reliable media sources. In case of confinement and available time, try to educate yourself in basic first aid techniques to provide medical care for minor injuries, as well as personal defense or combat techniques. Be prepared to adjust your plans as needed based on the evolving situation.

Remember that each situation is unique, and there's no definitive guide for all circumstances. You'll need to be psychologically flexible and prepared for the unexpected.

CHAPTER 17

A future with extraterrestrial life

The possibility of a future with extraterrestrial life raises a series of complex dilemmas that should be studied, analyzed, and reflected upon in action plans to be resorted to if necessary. It's a matter of such magnitude that I would dare to assert that, even if they remain concealed, extraterrestrial life forms most likely exist and are well-guarded.

First and foremost, we should explore various perspectives on how relationships and interactions between humanity and extraterrestrial civilizations might occur and, in turn, how they could influence our development and destiny as a species.

To do this, I would propose two possible alternatives that, as we've seen in previous chapters, would be predefined and lead to either detrimental or beneficial consequences.

Firstly, addressing the scenario in which contact with aliens is not amicable and thus hostile, we would face a series of highly unfavorable consequences for the human race.

An extraterrestrial invasion that hasn't been effectively managed from its inception could result in violent conflicts and widespread destruction. If the invaders are technologically superior, they could cause significant damage to various infrastructures, cities, towns, and ultimately the human population. As a consequence of this potential superiority, we could be subjugated and lose autonomy and freedom. The invaders might impose their will and system of governance upon us. There would be forced mass displacements of populations, leading to refugee crises and humanitarian problems. Global economic crisis would ensue. The destruction of infrastructure and resources would lead to recession, massive unemployment, and shortages of basic necessities, potentially sparking civil conflicts over their acquisition. We would descend into a social collapse marked by chaos and anarchy following the collapse of different social structures and systems of governance.

Depending on the technology employed by the invaders, there could be a significant impact on the Earth's environment. Advanced weaponry or geological changes could result in natural or environmental disasters, further complicating life on our planet.

In essence, all resources and attention would be redirected towards defense and survival. We would essentially regress to ancestral times where survival of the fittest and every person for themselves would rule.

Secondly, adopting a more optimistic view and assuming the scenario where contact with aliens is peaceful, a series of benefits would emerge, provided that society also responds positively and without disturbances to the news.

We would likely enjoy technological advancements. An advanced extraterrestrial civilization could share such advanced technologies in areas like energy, medicine, space propulsion, and communication. This could expedite human technological progress and exponentially enhance the quality of life on Earth. Similarly, we would gain new scientific perspectives as they might provide us with novel insights and viewpoints in fields like physics, biology, and astronomy, expanding our understanding of the universe.

Peaceful interaction with extraterrestrials could also lead to enriching cultural exchanges, where both civilizations not only share knowledge but also values and beliefs, enriching the human experience.

The presence of extraterrestrial life could motivate humanity to expand beyond Earth and engage more actively in space exploration, seeking new worlds and resources, thereby stimulating space exploration. In this scenario, a new intergalactic ethics and morality would need to be defined, sparking debates on how to treat other forms of intelligent life, and crafting models of interaction and trade for new resources that could necessitate the drafting of laws and norms transcending terrestrial boundaries. It's essential to note that it could also drive the desire for interplanetary colonization. Humans could seek new homes in the cosmos and extend their influence beyond Earth, underscoring the importance of laws based on respect and agreements of non-aggression among different species.

Confirmation of extraterrestrial life could also reshape our self-concept, our place in the cosmos, and foster a stronger sense of connection with other forms of life, starting with those closest to us on planet Earth. Similarly, there's no doubt that future generations would be more predisposed to work together to achieve a more advanced and peaceful world, paying greater attention to sustainability and the care of our planet, recognizing the importance of protecting our home in a cosmic context. They would likely experience a renewed sense of humility and connection with the universe.

CHAPTER 18

Throughout these pages, I have endeavored to describe the relationship that exists between certain phenomena related to the UFO world and psychology, as well as the psychological and emotional impact that the potential upcoming communication of extraterrestrial life could have on individuals, communities, and entire societies. I have attempted to explain how reactions would range from fear, awe, and uncertainty to fascination and hope, and I have suggested that psychological preparedness and effective communication could play an essential role in our response and, consequently, in the collective outcomes.

I believe that after the supposed arrival of Jesus Christ on Earth, we could be facing the second most significant event in human history, one that will not only change the beliefs, ways of thinking, feeling, and acting of many but will also bring about similar changes at sociopolitical, economic, and scientific levels, prompting us to reflect on the planning of strategies that define courses of action fostering positive outcomes for the human race.

If they aren't already, mental health professionals will become much more relevant, providing support and tools to confront the complex emotional reactions that may arise.

Ultimately, I extend a challenge to the reader for the reflections presented here to mark only the beginning of a broader and deeper conversation with oneself. An internal dialogue that leads to a greater understanding of oneself and one's place in this vast universe. A moment for contemplation and meditation. A pause in this ever-accelerating world. May this book serve as a reminder that, in our quest for the extraterrestrial, we are exploring our own potential and our connection to all the mysteries that surround us.

Let us have faith and pray, but let us also act so that whatever form this discovery takes, we can not only minimize harm but also derive maximum benefit for all.

Biography of the author

Christian Druso Gistain Montolío graduated in Psychology from the University of Valencia in the year 2005. He specialized in Forensic Psychology after completing the Master's in Legal Psychology and Mediation at the Miguel Hernández University of Elche. He also pursued the Master's in Disability and Law at the Menéndez Pelayo International University in 2022. He won the First Prize of the Chair of Research in Applied Psychology from COPCV in 2010 for the work "Arbitral Mediation; Socialization in Youth Football." He is the author of other books such as "The Storyteller, How to Make Story" (2010); "Applied Psychology in Hospitality and Tourism. Keys to Earn More Tips and Build Customer Loyalty" (2014); "PSYCHOECOLOGY The Theory of the Past Future" (2017); "Psychology in Hospitality and Tourism. 2021 Edition. Achieving Excellence, Customer Loyalty, and Increasing Tips" (2021); "Meaning of Tattoos in the World's Mafias" (2023).

At the time of this book's publication, he works and advises various companies in the tourism sector in the human resources department.

Other works by the author

Psicología aplicada en la Hostelería y el Turismo. Las claves para ganar más propinas y fidelizar clientes.

PSICOECOLOGÍA La teoría del futuro pasado

Psicología en la Hostelería y el Turismo. Edición 2021. Cómo alcanzar la excelencia, fidelizar clientes y ganar más propinas. Significado de los tatuajes de las mafias del mundo

Thank You

Thank you for acquiring and reading this book. Your contribution makes it possible for me to continue writing or investing my time in creating content like this.